# DAWN
## OF A
# NEW DAY

# DAWN
## OF A
# NEW DAY

PRECIOUS CARTER

CREATION
HOUSE

Dawn of a New Day by Precious Carter
Published by Creation House Books
A Charisma Media Company
600 Rinehart Road
Lake Mary, Florida 32746
www.charismamedia.com

Unless otherwise noted, all Scripture quotations are from the Holy Bible, New International Version. Copyright © 1973, 1978, 1984, International Bible Society. Used by permission.

Scripture quotations marked KJV are from the King James Version of the Bible.

Scripture quotations also from the Holy Bible, Today's New International Version®. Copyright © 2001, 2005 by Biblica®. Used by permission of Biblica®. All rights reserved worldwide.

English definitions are derived from *Merriam–Webster's Collegiate Dictionary, Eleventh Edition.*

Design Director: Bill Johnson
Cover design by Nathan Morgan

Visit the author's website: www.preciouscarter.com

Library of Congress Cataloging-in-Publication Data: 2011923398
International Standard Book Number: 978-1-61638-486-9

11 12 13 14 15 — 9 8 7 6 5 4 3 2 1
Printed in Canada

# Table of Contents

# Throw Your Baggage Overboard

*We took such a violent battering from the storm that the next day they began to throw the cargo overboard.*
—Acts 27:18

*I* HAVE HAD MY fair share of storms tear through my life. My prayer is that I don't ever have to experience them again, but I know realistically there will be others. As much as I don't want to admit it, when the storms are over we end up in a better situation than before.

There are a variety of reasons that God sends storms our way:

To strengthen our faith

To grab our attention

To clear some things out of our life

Now I am not saying that these are the only three reasons for storms in our lives, these are just the most popular situations. In Acts 27 Paul is sailing to Rome, and in verse 13 the storm begins to form. We are pretty smart people and can recognize when a storm is about to transpire in our life. Whether we like it or not, the storm is going to hit; the true test is what you do during the storm. Are you

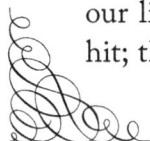

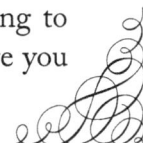

going to brace yourself for the storm and ride it out? Or are you going to exhaust all of your energy fighting against the storm so that you fall victim to it?

In verse 15 it explains how the ship was caught in the storm and could not head into the wind, so they gave way to the storm and were driven along with the current. Don't become a casualty to the storm! I have seen so many of our fellow brothers and sisters slip away because they didn't ride the storm out. They didn't recognize the purpose of the storm. Once you realize that you can't head into the forceful winds and give way to the storm, then that is half the battle. By no means do I mean give up when I state, "gave way." In this instance, to *give way* means to yield the right of way or relinquish position. Instead of trying to go against the turbulent winds of the storm, you just allow your boat to ride along with the storm.

After all, at this point you must recognize that there is a purpose to this storm. In the eighteenth verse of chapter 27, Paul tells us that because they took such a violent beating, the next day they began to throw cargo overboard. On the game show network, there is this game show entitled "Baggage." This show is another date connection-type show. It gets singles together, and people are eliminated based on the severity of the baggage they reveal. Some of you have some baggage that you need to throw overboard so that this storm can pass on by. God is trying to clean some areas up in your life to get you to the next level.

There are some things, habits, and people that you just can't take with you to the next level. God put this storm in your life for you to recognize the cargo that you must get rid of. I tell you, once you recognize that a storm has come your way, give way to it and determine its purpose. If you feel beaten up and defeated from the violent storm winds,

I encourage you not to give up but to lighten your load. "How do I lighten my load?" you ask. By relinquishing your position in the situation and yielding to the way of the Lord. You might not understand it at the time, but when it is all over you will understand the bigger picture. There might be some people you might not want to cut loose, but you have to trust what God is telling you. There might be some materialistic things you don't want to let go of, but you have to relinquish your position on that matter. There might be some habits that you have developed that seem impossible to break, but you have to yield to His will.

Remember, God has a plan for you and the plans that He has for you are to build you up and strengthen you, not to hurt or harm you. (See Jeremiah 29:11.) Trust that God sent this storm your way to clean up areas in your life that are holding you back from the plans that He has for you. Throw the cargo overboard so that you may sail through the storm into the calm peaceful waves.

# Seek Shelter from the Storm

*I would hurry to my place of shelter, far
from the tempest and storm.*
—Psalm 55:8

I REMEMBER A POINT in my life where everyone's opinion mattered deeply to me. As an adult I have come to realize that everyone is not my friend. I try to teach my daughters now that they shouldn't call everyone a friend—that should be a title given over time. I believe that time will allow you to see if that person is friend material. I can say that I have only four people that I can call true friends, although I have many associates and acquaintances that I am thankful for. There are only four people that I can truly share things with and confide in and know that they will give me sound advice whether I want to hear it or not.

Psalm 55 was written while David was in a state of distress. He was trying to deal with the treachery of a friend. To me it is sad to say that some relationships that you have engaged in will cause storms and turmoil in your life. You have to be careful whom you allow around your family, around your ministry, and in your life in general. I have seen it happen numerous times at places of work, in the community, and in some churches. You think that you found someone that you can confide in and associate yourself with, only to find out this person does not have your best interest at heart.

I am speaking to everyone, not just women. I have seen it happen to men as well. We can all be a bad judge of character at times. You never know a person's true intentions, so you have to keep your guard up in this area. Be careful what you share with people; everyone's not meant to know the intimate details of your struggles or the vision God has given you. People will see the success and blessings that God has poured into your life, and they will get envious and jealous because they want what you have instead of seeking their own blessing. The worst part is that sometimes it can be your own family causing you distress.

David sought the Lord so desperately in the psalm that he pleaded with Him. Psalm 55:8 is definitely a verse that you can turn to, to help you feel safe and secure in the Lord's arms. David expresses that he would hurry to his place of shelter. A shelter is a place that will cover and protect you. I felt intrigued to dig deeper to get some other meanings of the word *cover*. Outside of the obvious definition, I wanted to see the other definitions for myself. One definition stated, "To guard from attack." That is perfect because I immediately thought of God's covering over me guarding my life from the attack of the enemy. I remember my parents always praying over us before we went to school. They would always ask for the Lord to cover us with His protection as we went to school or other extracurricular activities. They would scare me by saying not to go anywhere that I had no business going because I would be outside of God's covering. This is the same method-ology of thinking that David is expressing right here; he knows that to be protected from the attack of his old friend turned enemy, he had to run to his shelter, which was into the arms of God. David was a man after God's own heart and he knew how to capture it, which is why he ended up writing the majority of Psalms.

Although David was going through distress, he did not let his situation cloud his judgment. He realized that he needed to get far from this situation. The end of the verse states that at his place of shelter he would be "far from the tempest and storm." That is what you have to rec-ognize; when someone else is deliberately trying to stir up a storm in your life, you need to run towards God's arms and get far away from the person that is trying to entice you to do wrong.

I want to remind you that everyone is not on your side. They are not always going to want to see you do well, and they are not always going to like you or what you stand for. I told my preteen daughter not to try to be a people pleaser; either people are going to like you for who you are or they are not. And it is okay if they don't like you; look at how many people didn't like Jesus when He walked the Earth. That didn't stop Him from doing His ministry or fulfilling His purpose. I encourage you today to first follow David's advice in regards to hurrying to a place of refuge to get far away from the storm. I really encourage you to follow Jesus' example of not allowing people's opinions to affect your ministry and purpose that God has for you in His kingdom.

# God Will Calm Your Storm

*He stilled the storm to a whisper; the*
*waves of the sea were hushed.*
—PSALM 107:29

To BE IN distress means to be in a state of danger or desperate need. I have noticed that no one can calm the storm but the Lord. A storm is uncontrollable to man. Only God can still the storm for you. I was reviewing Psalm 107:28–30, and it enlightened me on a few things. There are many situations that can put your mind in distress. When we allow ourselves to be stressed, we put our mind in a state of danger. When we become stressed, we begin to worry and allow the situation to control us instead of us getting control of the situation.

The best way to get control of a situation is to turn it over to the Lord. In verse 28 it states that they cried out to the Lord and He brought them out of distress. God wants you to depend upon Him and seek Him for help. Cry out with a loud voice, and the Lord will hear your cry. Those of us who are mothers know our children's cry. We could be at the playground and distinguish our child's cry from

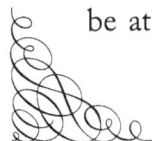

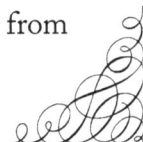

all of the other children. It is the same way with God; He can distinguish your cry from all of the chaos in the world and run to your side immediately, just like a parent responding to their child when they have fallen down and hurt themselves.

The key to coming out of distress is that you must cry out. By crying out you are asking the Lord to deliver you out of the situation. God doesn't want to see any of His children in desperate need or danger. With one command God can take a storm that is causing violent and turbulent waves and still it to a whisper and bring those waves to a hush. Please understand the severity in this illustration; with one command God can take your situation and turn it around before you can completely understand what took place. One minute you will be in your prayer closet crying out to the Lord because you can't stand to face the situation anymore, and then no quicker than you are drying your eyes with some tissue, you are receiving word that the storm just vanished.

In verse 30 it tells us, "They were glad when it grew calm, and he guided them to their desired haven." That's when the peace comes. Once the storm grows calm, He will lead you to the place that you desire. And not just any ole place, but a place that offers favorable opportunities and conditions. I urge you to not try to endure the storm alone; it will only put you in a state of danger. When you cry out to God, He will hear your cry and immediately deliver you out of that situation. Only He can calm the storm and cause the waves to cease. After the storm is over is when your blessing will begin. He will lead you in the direction of where your desires are and that will give you opportunities that are going to work out in your favor.

I encourage you to begin to develop a mindset that

you are going to get control of whatever storm is tearing through your life by turning it over to the Lord. The only way to turn it over to the Lord is to cry out with a loud voice. Humble yourself so that He may see the desires of your heart. Sit back and allow the Lord to guide you to that place of refuge. It is at that desirable place where you are going to find tranquility and blessings.

# Let Jesus Speak to Your Storm

*He replied, "You of little faith, why are you so
afraid?" Then he got up and rebuked the winds
and the waves, and it was completely calm.*
—MATTHEW 8:26

M

Y DAUGHTER AND I were flying back from one
of her photo shoots. I had to go to the restroom
on the plane; and wouldn't you know, as soon
as I closed the bathroom door, we started experiencing
extreme turbulence. I am thinking to myself, "Oh, Lord,
what am I going to do?" What would I do if there was an
emergency with the plane and I am stuck in the restroom?
I chuckled to myself as I looked in the mirror and with
all confidence stated, "Nothing is going to happen to this
plane because I am on it. I've got the Lord's work to do, so
we are going to be fine." Besides, I had prayed before we
took off from the ground (as I always do). I have no clue
where that mindset came from, but it worked; and I thank
the Lord, because that turbulence ceased as soon as I went
back to my seat.

I haven't always been that calm when the plane hits

the air pockets. I can tell you some stories. One time in particular was when I was coming back to the U.S. with my grandmother and brother, I had fallen asleep due to it being an eight-hour flight. Well, I happened to awake from my sleep due to a very rough landing; but I wasn't aware we had landed because my eyes were still closed. I squeezed the armrests with all my might and shouted, "Oh, my God! Oh, my God! We're going down! Lord, we're going down!" You can just imagine how embarrassed I was to open my eyes to my brother giggling, my grandmother looking at me in confusion, and everyone around me just glancing with blank stares.

In Matthew 8:23–26, the disciples must have looked the same way I looked: *crazy!* Here they are on a boat with Jesus, who is sleeping through the storm. The waves are tossing the boat back and forth and brushing water over the rails onto the deck. The disciples run to the Lord and shout, probably in the same deranged way I did, "Lord, save us! We're going to drown!" (v. 25). I am certain the Lord is probably frustrated at this point, thinking to Himself that the boat isn't going anywhere because He is on it and He still has a purpose to fulfill on the earth. Yet He asks them where their faith is and why are they afraid.

I can tell you from experience where their faith was: it went out the window when they saw the situation they were in. I can also tell you why they were afraid: because they saw the situation they were in and were looking at it with natural eyes. We as Christians tend to do that a lot. Our faith goes out the window when we look at the facts, and we become afraid when we see our surroundings. This is a bad habit that we are going to have to get out of.

We all know what faith is by now; but for those of us who do not know, look at Hebrews 11:1 (KJV): "Now faith is the substance of things hoped for, the evidence of things not seen." I can tell you right now that before then the disciples had never seen anyone command a storm. But somewhere deep down inside they had faith in Jesus, because the first thing they shouted was, "Lord, save us!" They just didn't have faith in the outcome of the situation, they thought they were going to drown because they had more faith in what they could see (the storm) than what they couldn't see (Jesus' miracles).

I encourage you today to not let your situation (the storm) control the amount of faith you have. Let your faith control the storm! It may look like the storm you are going through is overpowering your life to the point where you feel as if you drowning in all of your problems. That is why Jesus is our Savior; call out to Him to save you from the powerful storm that seems to be sweeping over your life. He will quickly rebuke the winds and waves that are tossing you around. That once powerful storm will become powerless at the sound of His voice.

In closing, I urge you to exercise your faith today. The stronger your faith, the more dependent upon God you become. The stronger your faith, the less afraid you are of the trials and tribulations in your life. I look at how far I have come from when I was that fifteen-year-old girl coming back to the states. The crazy thing is that my father was in the military and we have flown around the world all of the time since I was two, so I should have been used to it. Same thing with the disciples; a few of them were fishermen so they should have been used to those violent waves. But ever since that incident, I cringe every time we hit turbulence or rough landings. Now, I am not comparing myself to Jesus, but when we became born again, we became followers of Christ. Being Christians is all about developing a Christ-like mind. So over that weekend, I had to tap into this scripture (which God had given me two weeks earlier) and allow my faith to take control of that situation up in the air. You can apply the same principle in your life today. Just trust and believe in your Savior, Jesus Christ, and that God has a plan for you. Just know that no storm is going to stop you from fulfilling your destiny and purpose that God has for you to advance His kingdom.

# God Sometimes Sends the Storm

*Then the Lord sent a great wind on the sea, and such a violent storm arose that the ship threatened to break up.*
—Jonah 1:4

E HAVE ALL heard the story of Jonah and his purpose of ministering in Nineveh. *Veggie Tales* even has a video out regarding this. I believe that it is a Bible lesson that is not covered enough. We have so many people trying to do their own thing as opposed to what the Lord has instructed them to do. Some do not realize that they are not obeying the instruction of the Lord, while others don't feel comfortable with their assignment from the Lord so they come up with an alternative to try to compensate.

If you are not familiar with the story of Jonah, please read the whole first chapter of the Book of Jonah. It is such a captivating story that entails the start of self-destruction through disobedience. There are going to be things that we as ministers of Christ are going to have to do that we either don't understand or don't feel comfortable doing. One thing I can say about God is that He will take you out of your comfort zone. That is where Jonah went wrong,

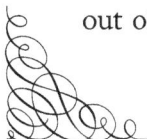

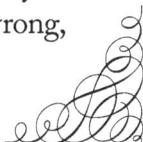

he was uncomfortable with going to Nineveh; and in fact I believe he was scared because he didn't think the people would receive him. To compensate and try to reason with God, Jonah figured he would go deliver Nineveh's word to Tarshish.

As ambassadors for Christ, we must be obedient. The word that God had placed in Jonah's heart was not for Tarshish. By Jonah trying to go and deliver a message from God to people that it was not intended for could have created confusion, and that is something God is not an author of. Jonah was trying to run from God because he was afraid and uncomfortable; but through his disobedience he was on the verge of creating confusion. The only way to stop Jonah dead in his tracks was for God to create a storm to capture his attention. Sometimes through our actions and disobedience towards God we create our own storms. It states in verse 4 that the Lord sent a violent storm that *threatened* to break up the ship. Now God could have easily sent a storm that *was going* to break the ship up, but that could have destroyed Jonah and that is not what the Lord wanted. To *threaten* means to send a sign or warning. That could be the purpose of your storm; God is sending you a warning to get back on track of the original plan that He has given you.

It goes on in the chapter to tell that Jonah confessed that he was the cause of the storm, and eventually the sailors threw him overboard to get the storm to calm. Let me tell you how good God is; not only did He send the storm to get Jonah back on track, He also sent a fish to swallow Jonah for three days and three nights. Now I want to get a little in-depth with verse 17 for a moment. If you think like me, I immediately was inquisitive in regards to why, first of all, he had to be swallowed by a giant fish, and then, secondly, why he had to stay inside the fish for three days and nights. I looked up the definition of s*wallow* because I knew my answer would be in that word (although clearly everyone knows what it means to swallow). *Webster's* gave the definition of *swallow* to mean to absorb. God will allow your situation to absorb you so that you can ponder and meditate on the purpose of the storm.

The purpose of the storm was to capture your attention and to get you back on track to do God's will. God sent the storm because of your disobedience, and He also sent the fish to absorb you. The following are a few examples of what this could be: (1) God gives you a certain amount to give for offering, but you are uncomfortable because it will really stretch your bank account so you only give half. Next thing you know your car won't start (the storm) and you take it to the mechanic and find it will actually cost double the amount God wanted you to give in offering (the fish swallowing you). (2) God wants you to volunteer in a ministry that could use your skills, but you don't want to give up your free time. God will send a storm your way to get your attention and make you uncomfortable so that you won't be able to enjoy your free time.

The reason Jonah had to stay inside of the fish for three days and nights is because the number *three* denotes completion. Although God was able to slow Jonah down, He needed to recreate Jonah inside the belly of the fish. By the time those three days and nights were up, Jonah was ready to go minister to Nineveh because he was complete in his training and more appreciative of the word that God had given him specifically for Nineveh.

You can't run from God. Whether you are intentionally not fulfilling your purpose or whether you are trying to take a different course because you are uncomfortable with how you are going to be received by the people of this world, it is better to face the people of this world with God on your side rather than trying to run from God to fulfill your own agenda. He is not having it! As quick as the thought pops into your head to veer off course, He will surely send a storm your way—not to harm you but to warn you of the consequences of your disobedience. Once the storm is calm, He will send a situation to absorb you to complete the process of renewing your mind to get back on track for the purpose He intended for you.

I want to encourage you: don't have God send a storm your way because of your disobedience. We were all created for a purpose. Don't deter from the purpose for which God placed you upon this Earth. Are you a little uncomfortable? So what! Just know that if you are uncomfortable, then you are probably on the right path and something great is about to happen, because God wants to take you out of your comfort zone. It is only out of that comfort zone that you can truly submit to His will and ways and serve full capacity in your purpose. If you are someone who is trying to run from God or trying to bargain with God, then stop immediately! Repent, seek, and pray so that you may get back on track of doing the work of the Lord.

# In the Midst of the Storm

*These men are springs without water and mists driven
by a storm. Blackest darkness is reserved for them.*
—2 Peter 2:17

WHEN YOU GO through a storm, you are in your most vulnerable state. A few years ago, I went through the worst storm in my life. I had reached a state of loneliness, depression, and fear of the unknown. I just wanted God to take the pain away. I had no clue which direction my life was heading; all I knew was that I had to stay close to the Lord. If there was something going on at the church, I was there; if there was a prayer line, I was in it. Although I felt I had lost my mind, I was still cautious of whom I asked to pray over me.

Even though you may feel like all hope is gone, you still have to keep your spirit man guarded. Second Peter 2 speaks about false prophets and their destruction. We are living in a time that some will start preaching things that are in direct contrast to the Bible or start believing things just because they are acceptable to society. This isn't just people in the world preaching these false doctrines;

there are some wolves in sheep's clothing in the church. Keep your mind and spirit refreshed and renewed in Jesus, regardless of your situation and circumstances.

It states that these false prophets are like springs without water. What an awful thing to be classified as! You know the whole purpose of a spring is to be a source of water. To be like a spring without water is to be like a vessel with no contents. I keep repeating this over again; each of us was created with a purpose. Don't surround yourself with people who have no purpose, those who have become springs without water. My mom used to tell me that "you are guilty by association and you are known by the company you keep." Surround yourself with people who know their purpose in life and are letting the water spring forth.

Although you may be going through a difficult situation in your life, please understand that your life does have meaning. Once you come out of this storm, you will have a clear understanding what the meaning and purpose your life has for the kingdom. But while you are in the storm, pray harder for that spirit of discernment and for God to protect you against those that come falsely in His name with ulterior motives. It also states in this verse that they are mists driven by a storm. I looked up the word *mist* because I had a little misunderstanding with the word. It is not to be confused with the word *dew*; they have completely different meanings. *Webster's* describes *mist* as something that obscures understanding; film before the eyes.

People will sense that you are going through a rough time in your life and how vulnerable and gullible you may be. The mist is driven by the storm. They will tell you anything to make you feel better, and their lies will try to obscure your understanding from the biblical foundation your life has been built on. Remember this storm is just another trial in your life that will add to your testimony and make you stronger in the Lord. Stay encouraged and prayed up so that you can see through people's motives. If they are in your life to help you get to that next level spiritually, then you will know them by the fruit that they bear. If something doesn't seem right to you, ask God to reveal that to you. The last part of this verse states that blackest darkness is reserved for them. Darkness can't mix with light! Let your light shine through the storm for all to see Christ Jesus living inside of you.

I pray that you have enjoyed these teachings about going through the storm. I encourage you to read everything that I have written about the storm. I pray that through the words that God has given me, you have an understanding of the purpose of your storm and the purpose that God created you for in His kingdom. I also pray that you take control of the situation by turning it over to Jesus and not allowing the storm to overtake you. Don't second guess yourself. If God told you to do it, then do it. If it isn't looking as you had envisioned it, then don't fret, because the Lord is not through with you yet. Keep seeking the Lord, and He will give you the desires of your heart. Pay close attention to the storm and learn from it so that you may come out of it a new creation spiritually!

# Give God Thanks

*At midnight I rise to give you thanks for your righteous laws.*
—PSALM 119:62

*J* BLOG ON A daily basis. My blogposts serve as inspiration to all regardless of where they are in their walk with Christ to help get through trying times. To read my daily blog entries, visit www.dawnofanewday .typepad.com. I write my blog early in the morning so that if people decide to check it the first thing when they get to work, then there will always be a fresh word waiting for them. My primary reason for doing this is that I want to give God my best, which by posting after midnight, I am giving Him the first hours of my day.

I am so thankful to God for His righteousness. It is His righteousness that sets us apart from the world. We were born *into* this world but we are not *of* this world. Once you make the choice of making Jesus your Lord and Savior, it is important that you make smart choices to set yourself apart from the world. When my oldest daughter transitioned from elementary school to middle school, I stressed to her the importance of making smart choices.

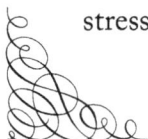

This is a critical age in a child's life. Middle school is the stage where peer pressure really kicks in, and it is easy for children to want to go with the in crowd.

When I think of how vulnerable middle schoolers can be, it takes me to Psalm 119:61–62. Get it embedded in your children's spirit that they will be tempted by people they believe to be their friends. Verse 61 states, "Though the wicked bind me with ropes, I will not forget your law." You see sometimes our adult minds can get just as vulnerable as teenagers. To *bind* is to confine or restrain. The wicked are miserable; they see your light shining so they try to separate or divide you from righteousness. Regardless of what gets thrown your way, no matter what kind of temptation you may face, you know right from wrong. No one can make you do anything that you don't want to do. If you feel as if you are tied up in a bad situation, never forget the laws of the Lord. That is what will get you out of the hands of the enemy.

The key to breaking loose from your situation is in verse 62. It states, "At midnight I rise to give you thanks for your righteous laws." No matter how terrible it looks to you right now, thank God for His righteous laws. It is those righteous laws that separate us from the world. Why at midnight? I don't know if you realize it, but when that clock strikes twelve midnight, it is a new day! Regardless of all of the mistakes that you made the day before, you get the chance to start the day off right. Praise God! You can praise your way out of any situation. So start off by giving thanks to God for His righteousness. Why? The Bible states that I have never seen the righteous forsaken! That is a promise that you can hold onto!

I urge you to grasp a hold of this; and if you have teenagers, break it down for them too. It is important to know that although it seems like the enemy has you defeated because he has you tied up in a situation, it isn't over! Let me give you some of *Webster's* many definitions of the word *rise*:

> To move upward
> To extend above others
> To attain a higher level
> To increase in quantity
> To take place
> To exert oneself to meet a challenge

Children of God, it is time for you to take your place as royalty; be the son or daughter of the most high King that you were born to be. It is time for you to move upward. Don't allow yourself to stagnate. It is time for you to go to a higher level. God wants to take you to a new level where you will be tremendously blessed. It is time for you to extend above others. God has made you for a purpose. Don't try to blend in with the crowd; stand out. It is time for you to increase the kingdom in quantity. Your ministry should be to convert others over to Christ. Lastly, it is time for you to meet the challenge. Life is not easy; success takes much hard work to achieve.

I want to encourage you to rise at midnight to give thanks to the Lord. It is at midnight that a new day begins. Forget about yesterday because you can't change the past. At midnight go into the new day remembering God's righteous laws and holding onto your praise of thanksgiving. It is your praise that will cause the wicked to flee! Remember, ultimately it is your choice of whether you will allow your situation to influence you or whether you are going to stand on the righteousness of God and rise at midnight.

*Day Eight*

# Be Prepared for the Bridegroom

*At midnight the cry rang out: "Here's the
bridegroom! Come out to meet him!"*
—MATTHEW 25:6

*J* HAVE HEARD THIS parable preached numerous times
from different angles. I think to get the most from
this particular passage, we need to really study and
listen to what God is speaking to us. In Matthew 25:1–13,
the primary message is about how no one knows the day or
hour that Christ (the bridegroom) will come back for His
church (the bride). We need to start preparing ourselves
now so that we are not caught off guard.

God spoke much more to me through this passage as
well. Remember, everyone was created for a purpose. Once
you have found out what you are called to do, it is your
responsibility to prepare yourself. The ten virgins knew their
purpose at the wedding banquet. They had the resources of
the lamps and jars of oil. Five of them decided to bring some
extra oil in addition to their lamps. The other five left their
jars of oil behind and thought the lamps would be sufficient
enough. Everyone was ready, so they thought. They waited

and waited and waited until they grew drowsy and even fell asleep. At midnight (the transition from the old day into the new) someone shouted that the bridegroom was coming, that it was time to come out to meet him. The five who were prepared simply turned on their lamps. The other five who were unprepared scurried around trying to find some oil. While they were out looking for their oil, the bridegroom came and took those that were prepared with him and the door shut behind them. The parable ends with the five unprepared virgins knocking on the door and the bridegroom turning them away stating that he does not know them.

God spoke to me at the age of sixteen, showing me my purpose here on earth. Over the years I held onto what God showed me, yet knew that it wouldn't happen right away. Well, over the years my spirit began to get drowsy and weary; I had been waiting for many years. God began to show me that I had to prepare myself. Although I knew my purpose, I had two choices:

- I could sit around with my Bible in my hand and wait for something to happen. And then when God does say, "Hey, I am ready. This is what I want you to do now," I am completely caught off guard because, like the five foolish virgins that only brought their lamps, I wouldn't be fully prepared. While I am scurrying around trying to prepare for what I have known for years is my purpose, I end up missing out on my blessing.

- I could start preparing myself now to advance the kingdom of God. To wait patiently; but

while I am waiting, I can start setting myself
up for the time for God to say, "I am ready to
bless you; and I see through all of your years
of preparation that you are ready to receive."
Through my obedience and stepping out in
faith to bring extra jars of oil to the wedding
banquet, I can be one who was wise and got
to accompany the bridegroom.

What frightens me the most about this passage is the
end of verse 10, where it states, "The door was shut." One
thing I have come to realize is that there will be doors of
opportunity in this world that will be shut on you. And
that is okay because where the world may close a door on
you, God will make a way for another to be opened. What
you don't want to happen is for the doors of heaven to be
closed on you, because there is no other way into heaven
except through Jesus Christ (the Bridegroom).

I took it a step further, since I have already professed
Jesus as my Lord and Savior. I don't want God to shut any
doors of blessing on me. I want to be ready at midnight for
when He comes to get me for ministry. We are all called to
serve in some area to advance the kingdom of God. Maybe
you are one that knows your calling and are just waiting
patiently for the right time to come. When is the right
time? No one knows; we have to wait patiently because
God shows up on His time, which is the right time. I want
to encourage you not to grow drowsy or weary while you
wait. Prepare yourself. Even when you think you have done
enough, keep preparing; because when God feels you are
ready, then that is when He will show up. And when He
shows up, you want to be ready to receive the blessing. God

won't use someone who is not prepared. He will pass right on by and close that door. Don't think that the work will go undone, because while you are out scurrying He will find someone else that was prepared to take your place.

One of my favorite John P. Kee songs is "Show up." It is an old song; and you can only imagine how I felt when the words came in my spirit randomly just before I wrote this. Those ten virgins waiting for the bridegroom to come had no sign. No one could tell them when the bridegroom was coming. They waited all night long; and then at *midnight He showed up on time*! If you have not accepted the Lord into your life, I urge you right now to stop what you are doing and pray the prayer of salvation. I ask the Lord to come into your life because, trust me, you do not want to be left behind. Jesus is coming back for His bride, and only those that He knows (that have accepted Him) will get through the doors. If you have already accepted the Lord as your personal Savior, then I urge you right now to start preparing yourself for your purpose on earth. Don't just sit back and think that because the Lord said it, all you have to do is wait. No, there is preparation that goes into ministry. You do have to wait, but while you are waiting it is your responsibility to be like the five wise virgins and equip yourself with the right resources. You want to be ready for when God says, "Okay, now it is time." You don't want to be like the five foolish virgins who were not prepared for their purpose and had the doors closed on their destiny.

*Day Nine*

# Cry Out At Midnight

*About midnight Paul and Silas were praying and singing hymns to God, and the other prisoners were listening to them.*
—ACTS 16:25

⟨⟨⟨⟩⟩⟩

ONE OF MY favorite hymns is "Just a Closer Walk with Thee." No matter how my spiritual life is going, I am always yearning for a closer walk with the Lord. Just to be close to God is my number one desire. I remember studying Genesis in depth back when I was twenty. It burned me up to realize how much Adam sacrificed by allowing the serpent to entice Eve and then Eve ultimately influencing him. I daydream and try to imagine Adam having the privilege of walking with God in the Garden of Eden on a daily basis. Listening to this hymn takes my mind into the Garden of Eden, as if I could encounter a daily walk with the Lord.

A hymn is a song of praise or joy. It delights the Lord when we offer praises up to Him because that is what He created us to do. What I have found over the years is that when the situation gets too tough for me to make sense of it, a simple song will do. I can be in the car in a stressful

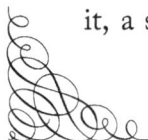

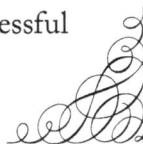

state of mind and a song will come on the radio or pop up in my spirit; and as soon as I sing a chorus, my mood immediately becomes joyful. Never fails, every single time!

Talk about seeing a situation through natural eyes; let's look at Paul and Silas. They were imprisoned and had committed no crime. Had Paul and Silas just looked at the situation, how it appeared, they could have just sat around and sulked feeling sorry for themselves. They could have given up and accepted defeat. Instead it states that around midnight they prayed and sang unto God. It doesn't say what they were singing, but we do know that they were singing songs of praise and joy. This means to me that they were not worried at all. By being joyful they demonstrated to the fullest that they had faith and trusted the Lord completely in this situation.

I also feel that Paul and Silas were doing the only thing that they knew to do. They didn't know what the future was going to bring, but their faithfulness in God brought about their blessing. In the next verse it tells of how a violent earthquake came about and shook the foundations of the jail. If you find yourself bound and chained in a situation, don't try to make sense of it, just praise God with a joyful spirit. It is your praise offering that will shake the basis of your troubles. Your praise will overcome the root of the problem. In fact, in Paul and Silas' case, the following verse it says that at once the doors flew open and everyone's chains fell off. Your praise will open doors for you that you never imagined could be opened. Your praise will cause not only the chains to fall off of you but everyone around you. God inhabits the praises of His people! Where the praises of the Lord dwell, that is where His Spirit is. It is a biblical principle: you can't go wrong with praising God. Get those songs of praise embedded in your spirit! When you feel as if your problems have overtaken and held you hostage and there is nothing left to do, arise at midnight and sing a song of praise with a joyful heart. It will be your praise that shakes the shackles and releases you from bondage. It will be your praise that causes people to stop and listen, just like the other prisoners did in Acts. People will see the peace and serenity that you have through your situation, and your spirit will help them get through theirs. It will be your praise that will cause doors to open that won't make sense realistically. It will be your praise that will cause other people around you to get blessed just by association (them being at the right place at the right time). Why at midnight? That is the deep and darkest time of day. You can't see in the dark so you have to rely completely on God. This is when you have to let your light shine the brightest. It is also the transition from one day into the next. It is the end of yesterday and the start of today.

You can't get much lower than being thrown in jail. I urge you to think about all that you are going through. I know countless situations can put us at a deep level of stress—a level that causes us to question why we keep setting ourselves up for failure; a level that makes you want to throw your hands up and say, "I surrender." When you get to that level, you have to dig deep. Dig deep and find those hymns and praise songs that have set the foundation for your walk with Christ. Cry out to God; He will hear your cry and deliver you from the camp of the enemy.

*Day Ten*

# Those Far Away Fear His Works

*Those living far away fear your wonders; where morning
dawns and evening fades you call forth songs of joy.*
—PSALM 65:8

JOY IS AN emotion evoked by well-being, success, or good fortune. There are going to be a lot of people that are not going to understand the source of your success and good fortune. We think that everyone has a mind like us when it comes to Christ. There are still those that are skeptics because they don't believe what they can't see. They are skeptical because there is no formula or way for them to prove it on paper.

I will be the first to admit that I am different and look weird to the world; it has taken me a while to get used to that. All my life I used to wonder why everyone couldn't like me. I felt I had the personality that gelled with everyone. As I got older and started getting to the point where I could minister and witness to people, that is when the confusion kicked in. One minute someone at work would be coming to me asking me to pray for them and looking for Bible scriptures to get them through the week, and then the following week that same person would be rolling their eyes at me or blatantly ignoring me. It baffled me and bothered me. I had done nothing wrong to this person, only tried to lead them to develop a better relationship with the Lord.

I didn't grasp the concept then; it took me a couple of more years down the road and a lot more people talking about me to understand. It became quite clear to me that everyone is not going to like me; and sometimes people don't like what they don't understand. People couldn't understand how someone like me was able to complete a five-year college program in four years. They couldn't understand how I could be a full-time student, full-time employee, mother, and wife. They couldn't understand how I had a new car. They couldn't understand how I could go back and get my MBA. There is a lot they couldn't understand. And instead of taking the time to get to know me and the God I serve, they chose to write me off. They chose to talk about me; they chose to make stuff up to fill in the gaps they didn't understand. Had they just taken five minutes, they would have quickly realized it was nothing I did but all God!

It took me a while to be okay with that. But guess what? I am completely fine with that now. You know why? Because I am a follower of Christ; and if they talked about Jesus then I know I am not exempt. They tried to write Him off and make up things about Him. I finally came to the realization that people fear things that they don't understand. And this verse clarifies it and goes so much deeper than what I can explain on my own. It states, "Those living far away fear your wonders." (See Psalm 65:8.) I took this to mean those living far away from God's ways fear His wonders. If you have not accepted the Lord into your life, or if you have not studied Scripture, then it is hard for you to accept something that you don't believe in. And when people start flooding their minds with questions that they cannot answer, then the spirit of envy and jealousy comes into play. People immediately began to wonder how a nobody like you can have the life you are living.

I want to encourage you to sing a song of joy. Rejoice in the blessings that God has bestowed upon you and don't feel guilty about your testimony. We don't live in a perfect world; and, I am sad to say, everyone is not a follower of Christ. Those who are not believers will not understand the joy we have in a time of sadness. They won't understand the principle of tithing and the fact that you can't out-give God. They won't be able to handle your willingness to not worry because you know who is in control and supplies every one of your needs. They don't understand because their life is so far away from God. Because they are not close to God, they fear His marvelous works and wonders.

In closing, let go of what people may be saying about you. Continue to live for God and let your light shine for all to see. When you are doing the work of the Lord, He will keep His hand upon you. No evil will come about you, regardless of what people are saying. People have a hard time accepting things that they don't understand. And if they don't have a willingness to want to know God, then let them be. Continue to pray for them, and pray that someone else may come along and water that seed you deposited. I know we all want to see everyone make it into the kingdom, but we can't want or force it on someone. They have to want it for themselves. Lastly, make a joyful noise unto the Lord for He is good!

# Find Joy In Your Day

*Satisfy us in the morning with your unfailing love,*
*that we may sing for joy and be glad all our days.*
—PSALM 90:14

*J* GET EXCITED WHEN I get into scriptures that refer to love. There are a lot of life lessons that have the best examples in the Bible. I am an avid believer that love is one of those principles where only the Bible can guide us. Every time someone mentions the word *love*, I always remember when I was in high school and there were tons of songs out there trying to explain what love is. Many stated that love hurts and how it brought about pain, etc. Being the naïve teenager that I was, I would sing along with these songs. It wasn't until I got married and studied what the Bible stated about love that I realized the world had it all wrong.

Psalm 90 is a prayer of Moses for the children of Israel. Moses is crying out to God, pleading to be satisfied in the morning with God's unfailing love. To be *satisfied* in this passage means to be given assurance of. Have you ever reached a point in your life where you know something but you just needed to be reminded of it? That is how they felt in this verse. You need that breakthrough and you know it is within your reach; God's love is going to push you through that situation. There is no love like the love of God, and it is written clearly in this verse. What makes God's love so different from those that have hurt me before, you may ask? God's love never fails! Everything that you need, God's love can be. Do you need to be comforted, healed, and lifted up? God's love can do all of that and more.

They wanted the Lord to give them some assurance of His unfailing love so that in the morning they could sing for joy and be glad for the rest of their days. They wanted to be delighted and pleased, and the only thing that could do that for them was the love of God. Many of us continue to search and search for something to fill that void, not realizing that the only thing that will make our life complete is God. My favorite worship song right now, "Nobody Greater" by Vashawn Mitchell, says it all.

Stop searching right now; I am here to bring your search to an end. You will find nobody greater than the Lord. There will be nobody that can love you like He can because His love never fails. There will be nobody that can do you like He does you because He will never let you down. If it is joy you are searching for and all you really want is to be happy, then cry out at midnight to the Lord! It is okay to ask Him to satisfy you with His unfailing love. When we are satisfied we get that sense that our desires are fulfilled, our expectations have been met, and our needs and demands have been supplied. The satisfaction that God gives us puts an end to our wants and desire to be loved by the world.

As Christians it is our responsibility to go out in the

world and demonstrate the love of God. We are ambassadors for Christ and need to show those that are hurting that there is a love that is greater than the love any person can offer. We need to display God's love for all to see. Can you imagine everyone in the world being joyful and glad? Remember that 1960s song, "What the World Needs Now Is Love"? Well, Hal David truly did get it almost right. What the world needs now is God's love.

# God Seeks True Worshipers

*Yet a time is coming and has now come when the true
worshipers will worship the Father in spirit and truth,
for they are the kind of worshipers the Father seeks.*
—John 4:23

M Y FAVORITE PART of the service is praise and
worship. It has nothing really to do with the
musical aspect, but the fact that I can close my
eyes and lift my hands and feel as if I am the only one in
the sanctuary reaching for God's glory. If you have never
had that true worship experience where you left praise and
worship feeling you have experienced God, I encourage
you to truly seek in your heart to desire an experience such
as this.

God created us to praise and worship Him. That is
our main purpose here on earth. Sometimes I think we
lose sight of that. We tend to just praise God seasonally.
There are some of us that praise Him while things are
going great in our life. There are others that praise God
through bad times. Lastly, there are that select few that
do praise God through any circumstance. I believe a lot of

times we get so caught up in our lives that we don't recognize our own habitual routines.

Years ago I was a seasonal worshiper. I would only be on fire for God while things were going great in my life. Now, that is not to say that I shut God out of my life; when I was going through trials and tribulations, I would pray through these bad times. But I was not consistent with my worship through any circumstance. It wasn't until a few years ago when I was completely knocked down into a pit that I couldn't dig myself out of that I realized praying wasn't my only defense mechanism. Through my personal time with God, I realized that sometimes all it took was praise and worship. At this point in my life, the only time I felt comfort and peace was when I sang a simple song of worship to the Lord, crying out how desperately I needed Him.

True worship is when you let yourself go and don't care who is staring. True worship is when you are not doing it for show. True worship is when you tear the walls down and become transparent and honest with yourself and God. It is in that secret place where you are able to go into the spiritual realm to have that one-on-one time with the Lord and to bask in the glory of His presence. When I am in that worship state, I envision myself in the throne room just offering up songs of praise to the Lord. John 4:23 is referencing true worship. It states that the time has come for true worshipers to worship the Lord in spirit and truth. What really stands out to me in this verse is the last part that states true worshipers are the kind of worshipers that God seeks.

Isn't that a beautiful thing to know that God is seeking the same thing you are searching to have? God desires that Shekinah glory experience as well. He desires it so much that He is seeking it out. Now is the time to put everything aside and focus more on developing a consistent worship experience. Regardless of what season you are in at this point in your life, set aside some time to just offer up praise and worship to the Lord. Don't wait until Sunday service or Wednesday night Bible study to be led into praise and worship. Look back and ask yourself, "What is my worship habit? Do I praise Him only when He blesses me? Do I just call Him when I need Him?"

If any of these situations apply to you, make it a point to try to seek out the ultimate worship experience. Sometimes we can get so consumed with life's situations that we do not understand the habits that we've developed. Now that it has been brought to your attention, make an effort to change! Get it in your heart and spirit to not be a seasonal worshiper any longer, but to be a true worshiper. Make it your heart's desire to want to be the one that God seeks. When you worship Him in spirit and in truth, your circumstances and situations begin to change. It is in spirit and truth that He reveals things to you.

*Day Thirteen*

# Seek the Lord's Glory

*Glory in his holy name; let the hearts of
those who seek the Lord rejoice.*
—1 Chronicles 16:10

❧

*R*EAD 1 Chronicles 16:9–11. These particular verses are psalms of David. Here we are instructed to sing praises to the Lord and tell of His marvelous works. We are also encouraged to look to the strength of the Lord and seek His face always.

I am going to backtrack through this particular passage. When I think of seeking His face, I am immediately taken back to the Old Testament in Exodus 33 when Moses pleaded with the Lord to see His glory. Moses wanted to see the Lord's face desperately, but God quickly informed him that no man should see His face and live. Even after God had spoken, Moses still was not content; but God could see the desire in Moses' heart. While Moses was not able to see the face of the Lord, God hid him in the cleft of the rock and covered Moses as He passed by so that he could see the back of God.

God wants to do the same for you! He will keep you

in the safety of the cleft of the rock while His hand is upon you. You must always seek His face regardless of what is told to you. Here is the kicker: when Moses came down from Mount Sinai, his face was so radiant, due to the glory of the Lord and his time spent with Him, that Aaron and the Israelites were afraid to come near him. They noticed something different about Moses that they couldn't explain, and it frightened them. The same thing will happen to you. People will start to notice that you are not how you used to be; and it will frighten them, because it is something they don't understand or can't explain. God's glory will be upon you. And if they are not in tune with the glory of God, then they will be just like the Israelites and not want to come around you. It used to bother me when this first happened to me. My husband can tell you of numerous times where I would cry, "What is wrong with me? I did nothing wrong to that person, why would they mistreat me all of a sudden?" My mom would sum it up with a simple phrase, "Darkness can't mix with light."

In closing, I want to encourage you to get it embedded in your heart to seek the Lord's face and rejoice! You know I am not going to let a day go by without giving you a definition. It is not that I think anyone is not capable of comprehending; I just want to give you a visual. When I see it on paper that is when the juices in my brain begin to flow and I can see clearly where the Lord is going. Here are *Webster's* definitions for the word *glory*:

> Praise, honor, or distinction
> Worshipful, praise, honor, and thanksgiving
> Something that secures praise
> A distinguished quality or asset
> State of great gratification or exaltation

As you can see, God's glory deserves some praise, which is why David tells us in verse 9 to sing unto the Lord of His wonderful acts. It is a form of exaltation; but most importantly, it is a distinguished quality—our desire is to be more like the Lord. Ask for the Holy Spirit to fall upon you, because that is a distinguished quality to have. In fact it is such a distinguished quality that it will indeed set you apart from the rest of the world.

# Seek Knowledge

*A discerning heart seeks knowledge, but
the mouth of a fool feeds on folly.*
—PROVERBS 15:14

*J*UST LOVE THE Book of Proverbs! It really causes you
to go into deep thought to fully understand the message that is trying to be conveyed. I've been focusing
on *seek*. Right now is the season for us to set our selfish
needs aside and just make God the number one priority in
our life. Yesterday we spoke about seeking God's face and
allowing His glory to reflect on us. Today we are looking
to seek His knowledge. Remember we are *in* this world,
not *of* this world.

My cousins in high school sometimes come to me
for advice, other times I just check in on them and volunteer my advice. One thing that I tell teens right off the
bat is, "Life is hard!" Not that I am trying to scare them, I
just want to prepare them for the real world. Let's just be
honest, we all at one point or another have cried out, "Life
is not fair!" I know I have probably several times this year.
I always follow up with, "Life is hard, but when you make

God your number one priority, situations are a lot easier to get through than if you didn't have Him in your life at all."

This proverb tells us that a discerning heart seeks knowledge. Knowledge is a key thing to have; without it you are definitely lost in this world. People will try to pull one over on you, and not just anybody but people that you call friends. God gives each of us a discerning spirit. If you feel that you are naïve and gullible, then I urge you right now to stop what you are doing and ask God to sharpen your spirit of discernment. Discernment will help sort out the sheep from the wolves in sheep's clothing. Let's take a look at discernment. It is being able recognize or identify things separate and distinct with senses other than vision. We all know right from wrong; now we have to seek His knowledge to be able to discern what is right and what is wrong. What you so desperately want right now may not necessarily be what is right for you. People whom you have known either all of your life or for umpteen years may not be the right people for you to associate with. And to be honest, there is nothing wrong with disassociating yourself from someone. It just simply means that you might be at a different level in your life than that person is capable of understanding.

This brings me to the next portion of the proverb: "But the mouth of a fool feeds on folly." So, our word of the day is *folly*. *Webster's* dictionary defines *folly* as lack of good sense, foolish actions or conduct, or lewd behavior. We have seen a few of these people at some point in our life. This is the person that is so discontent with their life that they thrive on the misfortune that is going on in everyone else's life. To sum it up, this is the person that fits the "misery loves company" description. I personally want people around me who are going to push me to get to that next higher level, who rejoice with me when things are great, and who are there to help me when things are not so great.

When my daughter started middle school and I had this talk with her over and over again. "Make good choices, don't be so quick to call everyone friend. Surround yourself with people who have the same morals and beliefs that we have. Be a leader and not a follower." At this age they are not very good at discerning because of jealousy, envy, and other ungodly things. To be honest, I know quite a few adults who seem to be oblivious to discernment. Even King Solomon asked for more wisdom and knowledge. God was going to grant him whatever he wanted; but Solomon knew that in order to be a great king, he was going to need wisdom and knowledge to discern situations in his kingdom.

In closing, I encourage you to seek God's knowledge and get it in your heart. God gives you the desires of your heart! And keep away from those that feed off of folly. When you are at that place where you are seeking God's face and glory, you have to be able to discern between those that are going to help you advance the kingdom of God and those that are not going anywhere and don't understand God's purpose for you.

*Day Fifteen*

# God Knows Your Heart

*And you, my son Solomon, acknowledge the God of your father, and serve him with wholehearted devotion and with a willing mind, for the Lord searches every heart and understands every motive behind the thoughts. If you seek him, he will be found by you; but if you forsake him, he will reject you forever.*
—1 Chronicles 28:9

WHEN YOU SERVE the Lord, it is either all or nothing. God has so much in store for His children, but there are times when we hold ourselves back. Let's look at 1 Chronicles 28:8–10. Verse 10 states that the Lord has chosen you to build the temple. At this point David is talking to his son Solomon, giving him the plans for the temple. God has chosen you to help advance and build His kingdom. Now it is up to you to choose.

The Lord wants people who are qualified in the area of being sold out. Verse 9 encourages us to serve Him with wholehearted devotion and with a willing mind. This means to be loyal, devoted, and free from all reserve and hesitation. That means trusting God and literally diving in headfirst! A lot of us come to church to get fed the Word, and we are content with just sitting in the pews. There are some of us that have this preconceived idea that because we are in leadership, we can only teach classes or wait for our opportunity to get called up to the platform. Where is our devotion to serve Him with a willing mind? Believe me when I tell you that not only does God know your thoughts, but He knows the motives behind them as well.

Let's take a look at what *Webster's* says about the word *serve*:

To be of use

To be worthy of reliance or trust

To comply with the commands or demands

To put in

To furnish or supply with something needed or desired

To answer the needs of

Do you see where I am going with this? We are all called to serve; yes, some of us are called to lead, but we lead by example! When there is an announcement from the church asking for volunteers and that is an area you are great in, you need to supply that desired need. I remember clearly one morning at altar call a lot of the altar workers were missing. The pastor looked around for help, and those of us that he noticed were in leadership; he literally called us out and told us to get up to the altar to pray for those that needed prayer. What do you think I did? I complied with the command. I answered the need of altar workers, I was not going to stand there and look crazy like I am not in that ministry so I am not going. No, the best quality of a good servant is that they get in where they fit in. That means that no matter what area in the kingdom, they will go where they are needed. That doesn't mean that is your permanent place in the kingdom, it is just to fill in until the person called to that position steps up.

I believe that if we actively seek God, then we can serve Him effectively. To *serve* also means to be trusted and worthy of reliance. When people are constantly calling on you and you have become their "go-to" person, then that is a pat on the back for you because you can consider yourself reliable.

In closing, all I am asking is that you devote your heart to seeking God, because He searches your heart for your thoughts and motives. When you possess a willing mind and you have the right motives, God will allow Himself to be found by you. Don't get caught up in the hype, don't worry about being seen. Your gift will make room for you! David said it best when he told his son, "God has chosen you so be strong and do the work." That is what I am saying to you: be strong in the Lord and do the work—that is the only way the kingdom will get built.

# Jesus Seeks the Lost

*For the Son of Man came to seek and to save what was lost.*
—LUKE 19:10

❧

*I* AM CONSTANTLY STRATEGIZING ways of how I can get more involved in advancing the kingdom of God. I just love the way that sounds—advancing the kingdom! I was at Wednesday night Bible study, the first Bible study of the year. I went in there with an expectation; all throughout the night I kept feeling this hunger. I left that night on a quest, I had this desire. I was no longer content with my actions. I loved ministering to the children and planting seeds of the Word in their hearts, but there was a desire in me that wanted more.

I wanted to be directly active in helping the lost come to Jesus; I wanted to help those who had lost their way to find their way back to Jesus. I love being a disciple for Christ. We all must remember that when we accept Jesus as our Lord and Savior, we become His followers; and when we become His followers, we then are His disciples. As a disciple of Christ it is our responsibility to spread His Word. We are to take on Christ's characteristics.

Luke 19 is the story of Zacchaeus the tax collector. Back then tax collecting was a shameful job. No one liked the tax collector; they thought of them as crooks. In this passage Jesus wants to fellowship with Zacchaeus but others were questioning how Jesus could hang out with a sinner. Jesus simply answered that He came to seek and save the lost. Church, it is now up to us to seek the lost! We can't just go to Sunday service and Bible study, volunteer our time in our perspective ministries, and think that is enough. It might be for that particular season, but I am here to let you know that after a while it will leave you feeling that hunger. I did it for nine years. God was blessing me and I was blessing other fellow Christians; but then it hit me hard.

We have to go out into the world and seek the lost, wherever we are today. That means going out on your job, your children's extracurricular activities, joining the out-reach ministry, or simply striking up a conversation with the drive-thru teller or cashier or person standing in line with you. We have to stop hiding in the church and get out there and be disciples of Christ. We have to *seek* and *save* the lost. I want to get to heaven and know that I made an impact in leading thousands of people to the Lord. What a wonderful feeling to know that a fellow human being has been saved from the pits of hell, all because we took on the Great Commission and surrendered ourselves to allow the Lord to use us for His purpose!

In closing, I ask that while you are seeking the Lord, you take on Christ's characteristics and seek the lost. I am not saying become best friends with them, but just let your light shine for all to see Christ living inside of you. Share your testimony; you never know who it is going to touch. It is all or nothing. Make up your mind to become sold out for Christ so that the lost may become saved.

# God Rewards Those Who Seek Him

*And without faith it is impossible to please God, because
anyone who comes to him must believe that he exists
and that he rewards those who earnestly seek him.*
—HEBREWS 11:6

I CAN REMEMBER BEING fresh out of college at the age
of twenty-one and making a list of things that I
wanted to accomplish in increments of five years all
the way up to age forty. By the age of twenty-five, I wanted
another child, to be a homeowner, to grow spiritually, and to
have my salary at a certain amount. I remember consistently
telling my husband that I did not want to have another child
unless my salary was at that amount. Well, I had my second
daughter three months after my twenty-fourth birthday.
When she was one month old, I pulled that list out and realized that I was not at the salary. I was nine months from my
twenty-fifth birthday and just shook my head. I was thirteen thousand dollars away from my desired salary. I thought
maybe I should redo this list; but no, I wrote the vision and
made the plan. I was enjoying being a stay-at-home mom and

was thinking about extending my maternity leave another two months. A week later I checked my e-mail. In it was a letter from my boss telling me that I had been promoted, and along with that promotion came a 20-percent increase, which brought my salary to the exact amount I had listed on my "by-the-age-of-twenty-five" plan. At the time I was only twenty-four and a half. Nobody, but God!

Two weeks into being thirty, I haven't had a breakdown from crossing into a new decade. Surprisingly, I have been excited and anxious to see what the Lord has in store for me. I think my thirties are going to be life changing and will set a precedent for me and my family. I revisited my list, and here is what it stated as goals for thirty: to own property, to have another amount for my desired salary, to be in management, and to have my relationship with the Lord to go to the next level. Guess what? We own some vacation property; I stepped into a managerial position when I was twenty-seven (plus I went back to school and received my master's degree at the age of twenty-eight—not even on my list); and fifteen months before my thirtieth birthday, I received my desired salary increase (twenty-five thousand dollars)! We serve a God with no limits!

Spiritually, though, I noticed that my spiritual being was stagnant and just going through the motions. I am not going to tell you what my goals for the age of thirty-five and forty are, but I will tell you they are very detailed except when it comes to my spiritual life. I am looking at the description on my list, and I wasn't very specific. I mean, come on, "grow spiritually" and "go to the next level in the Lord" are pretty general. Why weren't my spiritual goals specific? Was it due to the fact that I was only twenty-one when I made this list? No, that wouldn't be honest with you or me. I knew better,

I was raised in the church. God had made it plain to me at the age of fifteen where my place was in His kingdom and confirmed it in my early twenties. There is no excuse for my generic spiritual goals! I have now revisited my goals and made them very detailed because I am not just content with the materialistic things that He has given me in this world. I desire to do His will and I want to be on the right track toward the plans He has for me.

Now to our scripture, Hebrews 11:6. This flowed a bit different because I wanted you to connect with what I am about to say. I want you to know that from personal experience I know what you are going through. I know that sometimes you look at your present-day situation and see through natural eyes what is before you. I know how it feels to wonder, *How in the world is this situation going to be turned around?* I know of the possibilities of wondering if you set your standards too high or if you are being realistic. Without faith, you have nothing! Our number one desire should be to please God. And the problem is, if you don't have faith, then you can't please Him. It is easy to say you have faith. It is easy to go to church on Sundays and midweek Bible study and put your "faithometer" on high for show purposes. Actions speak louder than words. It is great to profess the faith you have, but you have to follow up on that by living your faith. Believing that Jesus Christ is your Lord and Savior is a start; but you must stand on His promises. If God said it, then it is so! That is the bottom line—no ifs, ands, or buts about it. I don't care what the situation looks like now; if you received a word from God, then exercise your faith and live as if the promise is already here. That way when God does bless you, while the rest of the world is in a state of shock trying to figure it out, you can stand there and boldly say, "I knew it all along. God said it, and I believed it!"

I encourage you to see God's glory in my testimony. It was not because of anything that I did that He blessed me (with the exception of me being very specific in what I desired). All I did was have faith! I specified what I desired and turned it over to Him. I didn't worry about my goals, and I only pull that sheet out every five years. I marvel at how I am able to cross everything off of my list that He has done. God wants us to be dependent upon Him. You can't do it alone; turn to God and earnestly seek Him. It states in this scripture that He rewards those that seek Him and please Him. How do we please Him? By having faith in Him—*always*! Not part of the time, but all of the time. Seek Him constantly! I am going to recommend a book: if you haven't read *God Chasers* by Tommy Tenney, then I urge you to go to your local Christian bookstore and get it. It is an awesome book on the chase of seeking God. I first read it about many years ago and have read it twice since.

Lastly, if you have not written your goals and ambitions, I encourage you to get them on paper. You may have goals and ideas in your head but they are no good there; you must get them on paper. Be specific. Write down any goal that you can think of. Whether it is career related, physical (weight loss), emotional (becoming a better parent, spouse, etc.), or most importantly, spiritually, be as specific as possible. If you want to lose fifteen pounds, then write it down. If you want to be making $50,000, then write it down. If you want to be ordained as a minister, seek God and write it down. Once you have written it down and prayed over it, turn it over to God, have faith in Him, and leave it there. If you don't do anything else, stand on this promise that God has made to all believers and those that follow Him: He rewards those that earnestly seek Him!

# Seek Righteousness

*Listen to me, you who pursue righteousness and who seek the Lord: Look to the rock from which you were cut and to the quarry from which you were hewn.*
—Isaiah 51:1

WE SHOULD ALL try to live a life in pursuit of righteousness. Every time I hear the word *righteousness*, I think of Psalm 37:25, especially the part that refers to never seeing the righteous forsaken. It was another promise from God that I was able to hang onto because I never wanted to feel forsaken. This scripture encouraged me to pursue righteousness so that God's hand would remain upon me. What is righteousness? Was I seeking it correctly, and did I need to do anything extra to ensure that I was considered a righteous person?

Well, *Webster*'s describes *righteous* as being free from guilt and sin, morally right, following divine and moral law. The first thing I thought of when I saw "divine and moral law" was the Ten Commandments. You can't get any more divine than that; after all, the Ten Commandments were given directly to Moses for the Israelites from God

Himself. Next I noticed the "free from guilt and sin." This really stuck out to me because there are so many of us that have not been able to let go of our past, so we allow the guilt to eat away at us. Here is where the righteousness of the Lord comes into play. Once we repent and ask the Lord to forgive us, we are required to forgive ourselves, which in turn allows us to be free from the guilt of the sin that was holding us back. The more you pursue and seek the Lord, the more this will get embedded in your spirit. Your morals will outweigh anything this world will throw at you to try, and tempt you with.

When in doubt, "look to the rock from which you are cut." The process for cutting a rock is very intricate. It entails many stages, but one important factor is that the stone that is cut from the rock does not lose its attributes. A rock represents firmness, foundation, and support. When you go through the process, it can be discouraging because the situation gets so tough that the finish line seems impossible to reach. When all else fails, look at the Rock from which you were cut. See the righteousness in the foundation and the support which Jesus gave when He died for our sins on Calvary. That great demonstration of love on the Cross is strong enough to free anyone from guilt and sin.

The end of the verse states: "and to the quarry from which you were hewn." One thing I have learned about God is that nothing is going to come easy. You ask for knowledge and wisdom, but you are not going to wake up one day with the ability to understand and know everything. You have to research and develop God's understanding to interpret the Word. That is why I am constantly in the dictionary looking up words, such as *quarry*, to develop a better understanding and to learn what it is God wants me to attain. The word *quarry* really caused me to dig deep.

*Quarry* means a rich source open excavation used to obtain building stone. *Excavation* is a cavity formed by cutting or digging. In this scripture, *quarry* can be believed to mean the cavity from which a building stone was cut or dug up. That is what we are: the building stone. The Lord wants to use each building stone to build up His kingdom. But it is not that simple. That last word, *hewn*, means to be crudely formed. Crude means rough! Never forget the road that you had to take to righteousness. It is your testimony. It is your responsibility to use it in building the kingdom.

In closing, continue to pursue and seek the righteousness of God. Whenever you are feeling down and unsure, just remember the Rock from which you were cut—the strength and foundation you received when you first gave your life to Christ. Remember the quarry from which you were hewn. Look back at all of the cutting and digging the Lord had to do to get you in the state you are today. Remember your purpose in God's kingdom. He wants to use you as a building stone to complete the kingdom.

*Day Nineteen*

# Seek the Lord for Everlasting Life

*This is what the Lord says to the house*
*of Israel: "Seek me and live."*

—Amos 5:4

*I* HOPE YOU HAVE enjoyed learning about seeking. It has been a blessing to me in so many ways! There are times in our lives where God challenges us in ways that we don't understand at the time, but once we sit back and watch things unfold, it is amazing to learn how He allows his plan to unravel. God has given each of us life. I remember hearing the older generation say, "We live to die and die to live." I used to think that was a strange saying, something that they made up to cause more confusion for me to try to decipher.

Well, when I read this scripture I thought of that saying. I thought about what life and living meant to me and here is what I came up with:

> Journey
> Success
> Mistakes
> Obstacles

I was still a little off, nothing really clicked with me. I looked in *Webster's* and found numerous definitions for *life*, but there were two that stuck out to me:

To have a life rich in experience
To maintain oneself

OK, now we are getting somewhere. *Experience* is the key word that I was searching for. We are all God's children, and as our father He wants nothing but the best for His children. As a mother of two, I want top quality and great things for my girls. I never want to see them fail; and if I can help them get through anything in life, I would. A perfect example is when we thought there was something wrong with my younger daughter's health. I found myself sulking for probably about five minutes. I thought about the love I had for my daughter and how I would do anything to ensure her good health. I even thought for a split second, *Lord, please let her be alright. Take me instead.* Then I snapped back into reality and thought, *Hold on, I don't have to settle for this.* I spoke life over my daughter, and then I immediately repented for trying to negotiate with God. I know that I have the Lord's work to do and this incident was merely a distraction. I proclaimed that we would be a family solely about God's business no matter what the facts looked like, because truth is we serve a mighty God who already has each of our destiny's mapped out. Needless to say, we were literally worried for nothing. My younger daughter came back with a clean bill of health.

God's love for us is much greater than the love we have for our own children. He doesn't want to see us suffer and struggle. God wants us to live an abundant life. He wants us to have a life rich in experience. What you experience throughout life is what makes and shapes you into the character that you become. The definition also stated *to maintain oneself.* We have to maintain a balance. The only way is through Jesus. Yes, we are living to die and will die so that we may live again. I also thought about how we must be born again to make it into heaven when we depart this world. That made me think about when we profess that we accept the Lord as our Savior, our old self dies and we become a new creature in Christ with a new life. The Lord wants you to seek Him so that you may live. God wants to bless you in this life and the next. He doesn't want you to settle. I have come to the realization that settling is the easy way out. You settle when you become impatient and don't want to wait for the real thing. Don't settle anymore. Don't settle in this life! Don't settle for that job when God promised you something else. Don't settle for that house just because you have been searching for months and haven't come across the house the Lord showed you. Don't settle for that relationship just because you want to be loved and don't want to wait on the one God designed specifically for you. Most importantly, don't get fed up and turn away from God because He isn't operating on your time.

Cherish life! Be appreciative and raise your standards. Realize that God wants you to have top quality and the desires of your heart. Seek Him and you shall live. You shall live a life worth living. Don't get frustrated when things get tight; remember that your life should be rich in experience. And remember God uses your experiences to transform you. Yield to His will and know that in order to live we have to die. Let go of things that are going to keep you from serving the Lord with all of your heart.

*Day Twenty*

# Break Through the Darkness

*The path of the righteous is like the first gleam of dawn,*
*shining ever brighter till the full light of day.*
—Proverbs 4:18

To be righteous is to be free from guilt and sin by living in accord with divine and moral law. When you accept Jesus into your life, one of the first things you do is pray the sinner's prayer. You repent of your sins and you have become a new creature in Christ. What a wonderful feeling to accept Christ in your life! The next step is to seek His righteousness. To be free from guilt and sin from your past is what gives you freedom in Christ.

In this passage of Scripture it tells us that the path of the righteous is like the first gleam of dawn. In this world as a Christian you are to shine bright for all to see Jesus living inside you. Being a Christian is not easy and does not exempt us from temptation. As long as we remain on the path of the righteous and walk with Jesus, being able to resist temptation becomes easier throughout the journey. That path that we take will appear over the horizon breaking through the darkness. Everyone is destined for something. While you are on this journey, it is your mission to seek out what it is that God created you to do. Make it your mission to be the light that appears out of the darkness and becomes that ray of hope.

At the sight of dawn it is apparent that a new day has begun. The second part of this verse states, "Shining ever brighter till the full light of day." Let your light shine bright. We as humans cannot function without the sun. Our vegetation depends upon it, some of our power depends upon it, and we can't experience a full cycle of seasons without the sun. Do you see where I am going with this?

Life is dependent upon the sun. And what the Lord wants for us is to be completely dependent upon Him. Let the rays of Jesus bring warmth into your life so that you may be able to shine to your fullest ability. Your walk with the Lord might be like solar power and bring a positive spiritual force to those that are plugged into you. When people see a positive change in your life due to the Lord working in you, they are going to want what you have, and the fundamental entity of the kingdom will transfer from you over into them.

Light makes vision possible! So if you are walking around with your light shining bright, then you are making it possible for those to see around you. The blinders are coming off and they are coming to the realization of what has been missing in their life. They are coming to the realization that they can't do it on their own. They are coming to the realization that they have been living in ignorance.

In closing, I want to encourage you to continue to walk on the path of the righteous. To be righteous does not give you a pass to think you are better than others; it merely frees you from guilt and sin. Set an example through the life that you live so that others can be released from the sin that is holding them in bondage.

*Day Twenty-one*

# Light Dawns in the Darkness

*Even in the darkness light dawns for the upright, for those*
*who are gracious and compassionate and righteous.*
—PSALM 112:4, TNIV

*I*N THE PREVIOUS chapter, the word *righteous* was defined as being free from guilt and sin by living in accord with divine and moral law. *Gracious* is defined by *Webster's* as showing kindness, courtesy, and generosity. To be compassionate one must demonstrate a sympathetic mentality for others who are distressed. Those who possess these qualities will see the light through the darkest hours.

We all know what darkness is, but I deem it important to research the word. It is important to develop a better understanding of darkness because it isn't just the night sky. Here are a few definitions of darkness:

> Not receiving, reflecting, transmitting, or radiating light
> Showing evil traits or desires
> Lacking knowledge
> Grim or depressing circumstances
> Not clear to the understanding

As I stared down at these various definitions, all I could think was, *Wow, this is bigger and deeper than I thought.* There are sometimes that we as Christians can get so caught up in other things that we have allowed ourselves to wonder out into darkness. We have allowed ourselves to become isolated to where we can't receive, reflect, transmit, or radiate the light of Jesus. There are situations that we get ourselves into where our flesh creates evil desires within us.

There are times where we are in complete darkness because of our lack of knowledge or our lack of ability to have a clear understanding on certain issues. There are situations that we have allowed our emotions to drag us into the darkness because of the spirit of depression.

When everything appears to be going wrong and it seems as if your prayer life has become stagnant and it feels as if you haven't heard from God or your life isn't reflecting that of a follower of Christ, look to the Light. When jealousy, envy, gossip, or other ungodly characteristics start to develop within you, look to the Light. When it feels like you are out of the loop and lacking knowledge or an understanding on issues and situations and that lack is causing you to be in the dark, look to the Light. When I say, "Look to the Light," I mean to look towards Jesus Christ to guide you through the darkness.

While it may seem as if you are surrounded by darkness, just continue to seek the Lord. He will be the Light that dawns on your life and carries you out of the darkness. No matter what you are going through, remember to remain true to yourself and your values. Continue to remain gracious and compassionate to others as Christ was. Continue to let the Lord guide you in everything that you do.

## Day Twenty-two

# Requests Made in the Morning

*In the morning, O Lord, you hear my voice; in the morning
I lay my requests before you and wait in expectation.*
—PSALM 5:3

GOD OPERATES ON His own time. I have always been one to think, *God already knows what He is going to do so, why does it take Him so long to do it?* Sometimes our lack of patience can make us sit around and ponder question after question, as if we are pacing the floor anxiously waiting for God. I know there have been several points in my life where I have thought, *Okay, Lord, I am so ready for this blessing, where is it?* Looking back I can see that God's timing is always right; because while He *will* give us the desires of our hearts, sometimes those desires are not a good fit for our life at that time.

This particular verse tells of how David laid his requests before the Lord and waited in expectation. When you arise in the morning, make your requests known to God. Lay them at the altar and leave them there. Doing these things will show that you are turning your needs over completely to the Lord. What I mean by "leave them there," is to not worry about how the requests are going to be met, when God will answer them, etc. The most important thing to do is to wait in expectation.

To *wait* in this instance means to remain stationary. Be still until you hear from the Lord in regards to your requests. While you wait, it also states to wait in expectation. Look forward to hearing from the Lord. Look forward to listening to the assignment He has for you. Look forward to receiving what He has for you.

Patience will be the key to your success in the Lord. While it may seem as if you have been forgotten, remember that God has not forgotten. He has heard your request and is just waiting for the right time to reveal the answer and/or the blessing to you. Wait on the Lord and maintain that expectancy that He *will* grant your request!

# God Remains Faithful

*To proclaim your love in the morning*
*and your faithfulness at night.*
—Psalm 92:2

ONE THING THAT I proclaim to those that I minister to who are going through trials is that God is faithful and He cares. I believe that it is important to remind people that God loves them and cares about their situations. I know how it feels to be in that place of loneliness, where it seems as if no one cares about how you are going to make it through. It is not a good feeling to feel as if you have been deserted or abandoned and have no one to rely on. Once I was reminded of the love that God has for me, I quickly wrote off the feeling of being lonely because I knew I was not alone and that was only a trick of the enemy.

Just as a twenty-four hour time period consists of day and night, our lives consist of periods of pure love and pure faithfulness. We feel loved when God showers blessings upon us. We feel loved when we are in service and feel the Holy Spirit fall upon us. We feel loved when God sends a word of encouragement into our lives. It is easy to feel loved when everything is going right and the sun is shining.

When night falls, that is when our faith must remain strong. We have to stand on God's Word and the promises that He has for us. We have to remember that as long as we stay in God's Word and follow His ways, He will remain faithful to us. The Lord will be faithful in His promises that He made to us. He will be faithful in giving us that strong assurance that we are going to make it.

I just want to leave you with this to meditate on: without faith nothing is possible, but with it, all things are possible! Encourage yourself in the Lord through the good times and the bad. Proclaim the love that He has for you in the morning, and proclaim His faithfulness to supply all of your needs in the night. You are a child of God, and God wants what is best for all of His children. Honor Him and continue to exercise your faith even when things are not going right, and I assure you that you will start to see the morning light.

*Day Twenty-four*

# God's Love Keeps Us

*Because of the Lord's great love we are not
consumed, for his compassions never fail. They are
new every morning; great is your faithfulness.*
—LAMENTATIONS 3:22–23

O BE *CONSUMED* is to be used up or done away with completely. I laughed when I thought about consumption. We as Christians have to be careful in this world. People in general will use you until they have no further need for you. In other ways some people can be so enraged with jealousy that they want to completely do away with you in your career, financially, and even in your ministry.

Thank God for His great love that protects us from being consumed. It is through the compassion that He has for us that He keeps His hand upon us so that the enemy cannot destroy us. God's love never fails and neither does His compassion. Regardless of what we do, we can always rely on the compassion of the Lord to give us that extra chance to get it together. I love the part in this verse that states, "It is new every morning." We get a new start every morning. Regardless of how we ended the previous day, His compassion is new every morning! You may be thinking, *Wow, there is no greater love than that.* We can learn a lesson from this. We who are Christ-like must follow this example. Never go to bed mad or angry; but if you choose to, in the morning start fresh with that person.

Keep in mind that although the world is trying to write you off and consume everything that you put your hand to, it is because of God's love that we are not consumed. The compassion that God has for us never fails. Even greater, He never gets fed up with us. The compassion that He has for us starts fresh the next morning. This is a promise of God and through His faithfulness is something that we can stand firm on.

# Make God Your Refuge

*But I will sing of your strength, in the
morning I will sing of your love; for you are
my fortress, my refuge in times of trouble.*
—PSALM 59:16

AVING LIVED OVERSEAS for twelve years, I have
seen my fair share of medieval fortresses. A fortress is a fortified place built to withstand attacks
and keep the enemy on the outside. I had become fasci-
nated with how fortresses were built. They normally are
self-sustaining and include a town. Everything they need
to survive is behind the walls of the fortress; a bakery, meat
market, linen store, blacksmith.

God wants you to consider Him your fortress! Only
He can provide you with protection against the attack
of the enemy. He wants you to rely solely upon Him
to survive. When times of trouble arise, find refuge in
the Lord. To seek refuge is to look for shelter or protection from danger or distress. There were plenty of times
when King David's life was in danger or situations arose
in his life that left him deeply distressed; and the only

comfort he could find was running to the Lord to seek refuge.

This scripture states, "I will sing of your strength." Most of the time when we sing, we are singing because we are happy and glad about something. I urge you today to sing of the Lord's strength not only in the good times, but sing of His strength in times of trouble. Rejoice in the Lord's strength! It is through relying on His strength that we will be able to withstand any situation that faces us.

His strength is solid. His strength has the power to resist force. His strength has the power to resist attack. His strength has the power to endure. His strength is logical and moral. The Lord's strength is everything we need it to be in our time of weakness.

When night falls and the morning comes, his strength remains to carry you through. God's everlasting and unfailing love is what will secure your victory over the enemy! When all else fails, take a moment and sing of His strength and love. You will see your victory in the morning.

# Cry Out to God for Help

*I rise before dawn and cry for help; I*
*have put my hope in your word.*
—PSALM 119:147

HAVE YOU EVER been in a place where you felt as if you have no more tears left to cry? Have you ever thought things were so bad that there were no more emotions left for you to experience and that the only thing that you had left was hope?

Sometimes the Lord will allow our situation to carry us to a place to where all that we can do is have hope in Him. It is in our hope that we cherish the desire that He is going to bring us through. It is through that hope that we have an anticipation of what blessing is waiting for us in the upcoming season. It is through that hope that we have an expectation that our God will meet our needs. It is through that hope that we are confident that God is bigger than any obstacle that stands in our way.

The time has drawn near for you to rise up as you begin to see the light break through your situation. Jesus is that light waiting for you to cry for help. When we cry for help, it is a plea for God to take over and lead us in the right direction that we need to be focused on. When all else fails, have hope in God's Word. God's Word is our instruction to get through life effectively. More importantly, the Bible said that Jesus is the Word. Ultimately have hope in Jesus because He is all the hope you need.

Hold on a little while longer, He is going to see you through. What seems impossible to man is only possible with God. When you have nothing left, maintain your hope in the Lord and His Word. There is nothing greater than knowing that God has got your back. Your hope should rest in Jesus alone.

# Put Your Trust in the Lord

*Let the morning bring me word of your unfailing
love, for I have put my trust in you. Show me the
way I should go, for to you I lift up my soul.*
—Psalm 143:8

MANY TIMES WE get stuck in the valley and want
to find a way out. Our experience in the valley
can range from a couple of weeks to a decade
or the majority of our life. Sometimes I think our time in
the valley is dependent upon the trust we display in the
Lord. We say and proclaim that we trust the Lord and
leave it in His hands, but do we really trust Him with the
circumstance?

One thing I have learned over the years is that everything has a cycle. We know that there is daytime and then
it gets dark; but the sun doesn't stay away long, morning
does come again. Nighttime is a time of rest, but our day
starts when we decide to set the alarm clock and rise.
When you fall asleep at night, you put your trust in the
alarm clock to go off in the morning to wake you up so
that you are not late for work, meetings, or school. We

need to apply the same thing in our spiritual lives. When darkness comes into our life, we need to rest in the safety of God's arms. We need to trust that God will bring us safely through into the morning. The same trust that you automatically put into that alarm clock to function to wake you up in the morning is the same trust that needs to be put into God to guide you out of your valley experience.

Once you feel the morning come in your life, remember God's unfailing love and cry out to Him asking Him to show you the way that you should go. Let Jesus be your guide. The whole purpose of a guide is to lead or direct another's way. Jesus is the Way, the Truth, and the Light. In your time of darkness, turn to Jesus; He is the Light. When you are lost and in an unknown land, turn to Jesus; He is the Way. When you are confused and it seems as if everyone else is compromising, turn to Jesus; He is the Truth.

The key to your breakthrough is in the last section of this scripture. It states, "For to you I lift up my soul." (See Psalm 25:1.) When you lift something up you are raising that particular object from a lower level to a higher one. The key to your destiny starts with you. God is there waiting; He just wants your act of submission. Start by really trusting Him. Don't just say it, you must live it. Then put an end to whatever situation is holding you back, by lifting up your soul to the Lord. It is through this act that you are allowing God to raise you from one position to a higher one.

# Let Your Light Shine

*The people living in darkness have seen a great light; on those living in the land of the shadow of death a light has dawned.*
—MATTHEW 4:16

YOU MAY NOT see it now, but your trials become a part of your testimony. I know I certainly didn't want to hear that when I was going through my valley experience. It is evident, and it is very true. The trials and tribulations that we go through are to make us stronger. They are to build onto our character and cause us to grow. Those things become a part of your testimony because they helped you transform into the person you are today.

Sometimes God will place you in the valley to use you to bring others out as well. You would be surprised at the many people living in darkness in today's society. Just turn on the news or look on the Internet. There are so many people who are lost and blind and have no intention in finding their way. They have made a life that pleases them in the valley. That is why it is important that no matter what you are going through, you keep His Word hidden

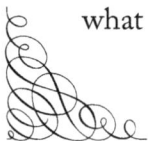

in your heart. Being a Christian means that we are Christ-like. God made us in His image. Jesus is the Light of the world, and even in our darkest hours we are still to let our light shine for all to see.

In this scripture it states that those living in the land of the shadow of death have seen a great light. Through your testimony allow Jesus to be that great light through you. We must minister to others who are still in darkness and give them something to look forward to. Let them know how you were able to overcome the same situation that they may be going through. Make it a point to shepherd some souls over to the Lord by sharing your testimony. It gives you a chance to reflect back from where God has brought you and provides another reason to give thanks to Him.

# Shine Like the Noonday Sun

*He will make your righteousness shine like the dawn,*
*the justice of your cause like the noonday sun.*
—Psalm 37:6

To be righteous is to be free from sin and guilt when acting in accord with divine and moral law. As I have stated in previous chapters, God rewards those who seek Him diligently and stay on the path of righteousness. When you are in the will of God, He will make your righteousness shine like the dawn. A lot of people confuse the dawn with the sunrise. While the two go hand in hand, they are completely different. We all know what the sunrise is; it is the sun peaking above the horizon. The dawn is that first light that you see breaking through the darkness before the sun appears. We are to be that light that the world sees to recognize the coming of Jesus Christ, the Son of God.

God is going to make your righteousness shine like the dawn. When you let your light shine, you will be bright by reflection of light. As Christians we are to be Christlike; our lives should be reflective of the life of Jesus. We are to stay on the righteous path and let others see Jesus living inside of us. We are a tool to reflect the light from the source to glow brightly. That source is Jesus!

Remember that you can try to achieve many things in this world, but nothing will matter if you don't have Jesus! Everything you do, do it for the kingdom. We are ambassadors for Christ; our cause should be done for the glory of the Lord. Some of you may not have found your cause yet. Your cause is something that brings about an effect or result. It is something that you are passionate about. Some of us may have many causes. Everyone has a cause; God created everyone for a purpose. Life consists of finding your purpose, your destiny, and your cause. Once you find your cause, He will make it shine like the noonday sun. God is faithful to those who love Him and stay on the righteous path. He gives us the desires of our hearts, and He knows everyone's motives behind their actions. The noonday sun is normally when the sun is at its highest elevation in the sky. I don't know about you, but I get ecstatic to know that my God has plans for my cause to be elevated high for all to see.

In closing, I want you to hold onto this verse as another promise from God. As long as you stay on the path of righteousness, that means staying free from guilt and sin while keeping His commandments. Then He is going to use you to minister His Word by reflecting His Light off of you. He is going to make sure that your cause will be lifted up high to that highest point for everyone to see. Stay in the kingdom; and if you haven't found your purpose or cause, continue to seek the Lord and ask Him to show you the direction that He wants you to go in. Take a moment to think about what you are passionate about and take a look at what sparks your interest and apply it to the kingdom. The first place to start with would be your testimony. Make it your goal and mission to make your cause about advancing the kingdom of God.

## Day Thirty

# Learn from Discipline

*Whoever loves discipline loves knowledge,*
*but he who hates correction is stupid.*
—Proverbs 12:1

*I* PRAY THAT OVER these past thirty days that you have attained the knowledge that you need to get you through whatever storm that has come and disrupted your life. We are never too old to learn, and there is always something new that we can attain from the Bible, regardless of how many times you have read it. There are a few things I want you to take away from this devotional:

> The storm doesn't last always
> Cry out at midnight for help
> Joy comes in the morning
> Seek Him first and He will give you the desires
>   of your heart

There is always a dawn of a new day. No matter what happened yesterday, the Lord loves you so much that He blesses you with a fresh start of a new day. Make the best of that new beginning and forget about your troubles in this world and focus on pleasing God. It is time for us to stop complaining about our situations and start thinking about what we are to take from the experience and how it is going to mold us into a better person. This scripture speaks to us about discipline being knowledge. Discipline is a course of training that corrects, molds, or perfects the mental faculties or moral character. A lot of times the situations we go through are a form of training to either correct or mold our moral character.

Face your storm head on and be willing to learn from it. There is no greater feeling than the one that you have once you have come out of a situation with a lesson acquired. We all desire to receive more wisdom and knowledge from the Lord. Be careful what you ask for, because there is always a process we must go through to get the results we desire. The process might not be something that we anticipate going through, but isn't that how it always works? Through the process, you must go through changes to lead toward a particular result. Those changes might be difficult to endure, but the end result will be well worth any storm raging through your life, any midnight hour endured in the darkness. The joy that accompanies the dawning light signifies that the morning of a new day has risen, making the whole process worthwhile.

As you go through the rest of your life after enduring this storm, I pray that you share your testimony with others about what God has done in your life. Live your life as an example for others to see that Jesus loves them and cares. Share with others that God can turn a situation to work out in their favor as long as they seek Him with all of their heart. Let your light shine bright like the noonday sun for all to see the goodness and mercy that God has for us because of His everlasting love.

# About the Author

PRECIOUS CARTER IS the founder of Dawn of a New Day Ministries, a ministry that seeks to help women who are overwhelmed by life's trials and tribulations. Through her ministry, Precious conducts Bible studies and seminars outside of the church walls to reach out to those in need of Jesus. She has a Bachelor's degree from Bowie State University and a MBA from Strayer University.

Her passion is to inspire women who are hurting and suffering from anger, bitterness, loneliness, abandonment, guilt, and shame, and show them that God loves them and cares. Her desire is to be that voice to inform women not to let their situation take control of them, but to take control of their situation by turning it over to the Lord. Precious' heart is to reach out to women all across the country through community outreach and conferences.

At the age of sixteen, Precious accepted the call God placed on her life. Through her experience as a life coach, mentor, youth pastor, children's church coordinator, and Bible study teacher, Precious desires to help people actively seek God to discover their purpose in the kingdom. Her conferences vary by city and are led by the desire and need felt in that region by the Lord.

Precious and her husband, Jean-Pierre, reside in Winter Garden, Florida, with their two beautiful daughters.

# Contact the Author

## To contact Precious Carter:

**Dawn of a New Day Ministries**
**P.O. Box 680706**
**Orlando, FL 32868**

## E-mail:

**info@dawnofanewdayministries.org**

## Or visit us on the web:

**www.preciouscarter.com**
**www.dawnofanewdayministries.org**